William Rankin Duryee

Religious Lyrics and Occasional Verses

William Rankin Duryee

Religious Lyrics and Occasional Verses

ISBN/EAN: 9783744784429

Printed in Europe, USA, Canada, Australia, Japan

Cover: Foto ©Lupo / pixelio.de

More available books at **www.hansebooks.com**

RELIGIOUS LYRICS

AND

OCCASIONAL VERSES

BY

WM. RANKIN DURYEE, D.D.

NEW YORK

ANSON D. F. RANDOLPH & CO.,

38 WEST TWENTY-THIRD STREET

1887

University Press:
JOHN WILSON AND SON, CAMBRIDGE.

PREFACE.

THE religious verses here printed have already appeared in various " poets' corners," — some over my own name, and some over the *pseudonym* of George Sharpe, as in the case of the " Via Dolorosa." " The Kingdom of Home " was a prize song on home, and may be found in various collections. All of merit these verses contain they owe to a father, mother, and wife, whose earthly love fostered and sustained the love supreme. God has taken them now to the higher home, and all that is left to me is to dedicate to their dear memory this little book.

JUNE, 1887.

OCCASIONAL VERSES.

RELIGIOUS LYRICS.

RELIGIOUS LYRICS.

THE ALPHA AND OMEGA.

THE seaman on a stormy main
Traces upon the chart his way,
And for the port he longs to gain
   His course prepares each day.

O life of Jesus ! be to me
A chart engraven on the soul,
Guiding through doubt and mystery
   To manhood's noblest goal.

And every wind the seaman hails
Which speeds him swifter on the course,
The helm he moves, he bends the sails
   To catch its utmost force.

O Love of Jesus ! in me burn,
That answering love within my breast
May duty, pleasure, sorrow turn
    To speed me toward Thy rest.

BROTHERHOOD.

I LOVE the Church, God's chosen home,
  All-glorious in His sight,
Firm on the Christ, the corner-stone,
  And radiant with His light.
Oh ! never from this soul of mine
  May fade this holy love
Till from the Church below I rise
  To greet the Church above.

I love the Church which holds the faith
  A Saviour's lips bestowed,
When through the three and thirty years
  Those lips with grace o'erflowed, —
Which finds in Him her only Priest
  The sacrifice to bring,
And, bowed in meek humility,
  Reveres Him as her King.

Apollos, Cephas, Paul ! not theirs
   The name she joys to own,
But deeper in the soul engraved
   The name of Christ alone.
And he who bears it, far or near,
   Is brother still of mine,
With me to feast on heavenly bread
   And drink the holy wine.

What care I, if by differing names
   Christ's chosen are enrolled?
One Israel still through all the tribes,
   One flock in many a fold.
Beneath their feet one way extends
   To shining realms above,
Before their ranks one ensign gleams
   With blazonry of love.

And sadly in these battle-days
   Some bitter voice I hear
Which fain would force from out the line
   A soul to Jesus dear.
" He followeth not with us ; " " His name
   From brotherhood we blot."

Still turns the Christ, with eyes aflame,
"Beware ! rebuke him not."

Oh ! if below with blinded minds
  The Word of love we read,
Like sullen children if we clash
  On rite and form and creed, —
When at the dear Lord's feet we fall
  To find His smile our bliss,
How soon the earthly strife shall fade,
  Lost in a love like His !

There, Luther's songs more ardent rise,
  There, Knox of fearless mien,
There, Calvin of the sunlit soul,
  Move in a peace serene.
There, Leighton of the holy life,
  And Bunyan, pilgrim tried,
With Baxter find the perfect rest
  Amid the glorified.

Then grant to me e'en now, O Lord !
  The brother's heart and hand,
Beside Thy feast to welcome Thine,
  Before Thy cross to stand,

Till Love shall rise as in the skies,
And in its burning glow
Thy Church in unity display, —
A heaven begun below.

THE RESTORER'S ADVENT.

THE haggard earth gropes on in sin,
  It learns but how to weep ;
Each pleasure carries deep within
  The pain to banish sleep.
Its gilded loads crush down the soul
  As faster speeds the day,
While robed beneath night's sable cowl
  Wait Terror and Dismay.
But hark ! in midnight moments still
A song floats o'er the eastern hill :
  The Christ ! the Christ, is come !

Strange song to thrill the weary soul !
  Whence may its music come ?
It is not blent with ocean's roll,
  Nor with the city's hum ;
But from the stars which heaven gem,
  Lo ! radiant angels bring

To shepherds poor of Bethlehem
  The song a world shall sing.
There first sounds forth the joyous strain
Which heavenly hosts might not retain :
  The Christ, the Christ is come !

" O sin-cursed earth ! we bring the word
  Your sinking heart to stay ;
A Saviour, who is Christ the Lord,
  Is born for you to-day.
For sinful earth He stoops to bear
  Away the guilt and shame ;
For you He condescends to wear
  A human heart and name.
Go, shepherds, view the glorious birth,
And spread the news through saddened earth,
  The Christ, the Christ is come !

" His palace ? View the manger's side.
  Friends ? Toiling men are near.
No pomp and retinue of pride,
  No judgment frowns appear ;
A blessed Babe, whose loving smile
  Turns swift where love is shown,

No kneeling soul too mean or vile
    To make that smile its own."
So sounds above the shepherd throng,
So distant dies the angels' song ;
    The Christ, the Christ is come !

Then Faith beholds the ladder near
    Which charmed the dreamer's sight ;
Then Peace, with balm for mortal fear,
    Stands plumed for world-wide flight ;
Then Hope flings wide the Eden gates
    Where sword of cherub gleamed,
While Love divine the entrance waits
    Of joyous souls redeemed.
Night breaks as beams in eastern sky
The glorious Dayspring from on high,
    And Christ, the Christ is come !

THE PEACE-GIVER.

'T was night, and on a stormy sea
  A toiling, weary crew
Heard from the hills of Galilee
  The blasts rush down anew.
Weaker each arm that strove to save,
  Each heart more faint with fear ;
When lo ! across the crested wave
  A stately Form draws near.

Human, and yet He walks the deep
  Unharmed where others die !
Strange terrors through the seamen creep,
  And quiver in their cry.
He turns ; afar those terrors flee
  As dawn dispels each shade,
For Jesus calls across the sea :
  " 'T is I ; be not afraid ! "

So when my weak and struggling soul,
  By storms of trouble tossed,
Hears from afar new surges roll,
  And deems that all is lost, —
Again One comes to still despair
  And check each hopeless cry :
" The sceptre of the sea I bear, —
  Be not afraid ; 't is I ! "

BETHANY.

THERE is a little village
    On sunny Olivet,
Where many saddened hearts have turned,
    And eyes with weeping wet;
For, through the veil of flowing tears,
    There may the mourner see
A Saviour bowed by human grief
    In stricken Bethany.

Nor hidden deep the reason
    Those tears divine should fall,
When hearts bereaved by ruthless Death
    Against the tyrant call.
That quivering frame, those weeping eyes
    Show what the heart must be
Of Jesus who with mourners wept
    In darkened Bethany.

So when the storm of anguish
    Sweeps on the soul again,

When Love's refreshing springs of joy
  Give forth strange draughts of pain, —
O Master ! all our broken hopes
  And hearts we bring to Thee,
Believing surely " Jesus wept "
  Our tears in Bethany.

Speak to us then, O Saviour !
  The peace earth cannot give ;
Teach us anew that Death has past
  For all that in Thee live.
And through the veil Thy hand has rent,
  May Faith, enraptured, see
A nobler life restored than that
  Which gladdened Bethany.

O village on the hillside,
  Thy memory how dear !
The voice of love the sisters heard,
  How sweet to Sorrow's ear !
From thee we gain what none have found,
  By quest on land or sea, —
The balm which soothes the broken heart
  In peaceful Bethany.

VIA DOLOROSA.

While I pace the narrow street
Trodden once by weary feet,
Where Immanuel bore the cross,
Where my gain became His loss, —
Teach me, Saviour, there to be
Truer follower of Thee.

From these gloomy walls of stone
Hear I yet the suffering groan,
Echoes still the taunting jeer,
Laugh of scorn to find Thee here.
Blinded hearts and darkened eyes,
Could ye so your Lord despise?

Not for Thee that cross was borne,
Not for sin of Thine the scorn;
All that on Thy head was laid
From the hour that hate betrayed
Till they nailed Thee to the tree,
Thou alone did'st bear for me!

'T was for me that brow was torn
By the cruel crown of thorn ;
'T was for me those nails were driven ;
'T was for me that side was riven :
All Thy wounds but wounds of love,
All, a grace divine to prove !

Who within this darkened way
Would not, Saviour, long to stay, —
Finding every heartstring move
Thrilling to the touch of love ;
Borne upon a mighty tide
Closer, closer to Thy side ?

Pacing still the narrow street
Trodden once by weary feet,
Looking forward to the crown
When I lay my burden down,
By Thy grace, oh, may I be
Truer follower of Thee !

EXPERIENCE.

I DEEMED, O Sorrow! I could trace
Thy features, and their meaning know,
As oft I scanned thy veilèd face
Through tears that fell for human woe.

How vain the thought! When thou didst stand
Within my own love-guarded door,
And for my treasure reach thy hand,
I saw a face unknown before, —

An awful face that bowed my will
In all the weakness of despair,
While sounded low, distinct, and chill,
A voice that seemed to banish prayer.

A darkness quenched the noontide day;
From all the world the glory fled;
The firelight fell in ashes gray;
The withered flowers of love lay dead.

No more I measure other tears,
Nor deem thy path, O Sorrow ! known ;
Alone thou walkest through the years,
Thy veil is raised to each alone.

But One thy utmost power has met,
And from thy bitterness can free, —
The Soul that bowed on Olivet,
And bore our griefs on Calvary.

CALVARY.

Stay, my soul, with conflict weary,
   By thy sins so hardly pressed,
Dark life's bitter way and dreary,
   Here on Calvary's summit rest !
On that central cross extending,
   Lo ! the Lord of Glory hangs ;
From His lips the cry ascending
   Tells of more than mortal pangs.

Yes, 't is He to whom in glory
   Thousand angels bent the knee ;
Now His sorrows tell the story
   Of a love divine for thee.
Thine the guilt that makes Him languish,
   Thine the sin that bows His head ;
Only by Emmanuel's anguish
   See the sinner's ransom paid.

Why, then, by thy foes affrighted,
　In thy weakness overborne?
Here the way to heaven is lighted,
　Here thy chains asunder torn.
When the storms of Justice, flying,
　Overwhelm the sinner's head,
Sheltered mayst thou stand, relying
　On the cross where Jesus bled.

Turn again, O soul! in gladness,
　Grateful love thy life sustains;
Cast behind thee all thy sadness,
　Sorrows now are changed to gains.
Sin and Satan flee before thee,
　Death, disarmed, can bring no loss,·
With the piercèd Hands stretched o'er thee
　As thou kneelest at the cross.

RESIGNATION.

WITHIN the darkness, where no light has come,
  Save where too-distant stars unwearied shine,
My heart cries out, though quivering lips are dumb :
  " Thy will, O Lord, be mine ! "

Though dear ones leave me and the home is rent,
  Than which no earthly home had been more blest,
A Power supremely good has sorrow sent,
  And on that heart I rest.

For I do know, — not think, but surely know, —
  From thousand tokens in this earthly frame,
Whate'er the blessing or whate'er the blow,
  LOVE is its Sovereign's name.

Accurst of earth and heaven the bigot's dream
  That He who gave the life and formed the heart,
Frowns on our love, however sweet it seem,
  And forces souls apart !

Far sooner let me follow fools who swear
    Man sits the monarch on a despot's throne, —
No rule above whose curse he may not dare,
    No will beyond his own.

Forgive the blasphemy, O gracious Lord !
    Temptations strong assail me in my need ;
Thou hast not Thine own blessed gift abhorred,
    Nor taught the woful creed.

For Love that claims Thy blessing is Thine own ;
    From Thee it sprang, alone in Thee can grow ;
With everlasting arms around it thrown,
    Death it can never know.

Life parts the loving not the less than Death :
    Death not the less than Life must own Thy power;
For saints above, as on the earth beneath,
    Gleams bright Love's trysting hour.

Love is but drawn from earth to heaven and Thee,
    Thou Sun amid the stars of lesser beam ;
Thy love with ours combined eternally
    In glory how supreme !

So here on earth Thou once didst leave Thine own,
    Though one was leaning closely on Thy breast,
A little while to wait in lands unknown
    Till they should gain Thy rest.

Thy will be mine, O Lord ! each parting make
    The hour of deeper longing for Thy light ;
So, gathering store for coming joy, I take
    My song up in the night.

DOUBT.

Dense falls the fog-bank on the bay,
 It veils each landmark of the hill ;
The drifting sailors grope their way
 With dismal bell and whistle shrill.

On rustic roads its darkness falls,
 Through which the ghostly shadows roam ;
Men shudder at the churchyard walls,
 And long to catch the sounds of home.

But lo ! the trees begin to creak.
 Blow swift and strong, ye winds of day !
One blast from you, and fog and reek
 Have fled, like fevered dreams, away.

 . . . . . .

On realms of thought a darkness sweeps :
 Men turn to monsters in its gloom ;
At hopeless graves the mourner weeps,
 Or quakes at spectres from the tomb.

3

No path below, no heaven above
　　With sunny truth to light the air ;
Here sounds the dismal sneer at love,
　　Here answer wailings of despair.

Whence come we ?　Whither do we go ?
　　What fetters these that bind us round ?
Must Wisdom's end be not to know,
　　And Life be quenched in graveyard ground ?

From heights above there comes the thrill.
　　O breath of God ! from out that height
Blow fresh and strong upon the chill
　　And darkness of this earth-born night !

One rushing blast renews the soul,
　　And fear and terror melt away ;
Faith sees beyond the grave its goal,
　　Love soars in song upon the way.

SORROW.

WE mourn not those who drink Life's genial wine,
  And while their pulses feel the warmest thrill
Lay down the goblet at a call divine
  For richer feasts which nobler longings fill.

Nor tears for those who, like the guarded flowers
  When deepest hued, are from companions torn,
As walks the Master in His loving hours
  Seeking the rare which may His home adorn.

We weep not when with sudden wrench the gem
  Is from unseemly setting forced apart,
To sparkle on a monarch's diadem,
  Or flash its rays on Love's delighted heart.

But constant tears for those who here must quaff
  Life's bitter dregs, or, fading long, must stay
To meet the Winter, while with scornful laugh
  A mocking world sweeps by upon the way.

Not thee we mourn, O friend ! as fall our tears,
    Thine is the rest, the glory, and the gain ;
We grieve that we, more lonely, walk the years
    And weaker turn to earthly toil and pain.

But brighter are the skies since thou art there,
    Warmer the welcome after parting tears ;
The farewell that we breathe uplifts the prayer
    That soon may dawn for us God's golden years.

EASTER.

O EARTH, cold Earth ! to life arise,
   The birds are singing round thee ;
Chill Winter in the distance flies,
And on thy surface, broken, lies
   His icy band that bound thee :
Uprise, in blooming beauty drest,
   As Power and Love have crowned thee.

O World ! accurst by sin and shame,
   Let light dispel thy madness ;
Life comes to renovate thy frame,
To burn thy dross by blasting flame, —
   Arouse thee from thy sadness.
A Conqueror stands, with kingly touch,
   To change thy grief to gladness.

O Soul ! unfettered at the cross,
   Yet in thy weakness lying,
Arise ! put off all fear of loss ;

To thee, earth's battlefield across,
　　A voice divine is crying :
" Gird on My strength ; thy life I hold,
　　To give thee songs for sighing."

For lo ! the portals of the tomb —
　　Unsealed in earthly story,
Where hearts have sunk in hopeless gloom
As friends have bowed to meet its doom
　　Through all the ages hoary —
Roll back for Manhood's highest heir,
　　The Lord of life and glory.

He stands in life no more to die,
　　Death's strongest fetters riven ;
Ring out, ye bells, the triumph high
In peals that sound to earth and sky,
　　The joy of souls forgiven !
Above the grave a new name gleams,
　　The Bethel-gate of heaven.

THE VICTORY.

CHRIST has conquered ! Hear the shout
 From the highest heaven ringing ;
Angel voices send it out,
 Loud the song of triumph singing.
Hell's dark host is vanquished now :
Place the crown on Jesu's brow !

Christ has conquered ! Lost, O Grave !
 Is thy hold upon the mortal,
Fled the fear thy presence gave ;
 Thou for life art made the portal.
By thy side the Christian sings,
"Crown the Saviour King of kings."

Christ has conquered ! Death's cold hand
 Never more the sceptre wielding,
May a world enslaved command ;
 Low he bends, that sceptre yielding.
King of Terrors, vanquished thou !
Place the crown on Jesu's brow.

Christ has conquered !   Visions bright,
　O'er the Christian's conflict shining,
Bring to vales of darkness light,
　Give each cloud its silver lining.
Hark ! from closing lips it rings,
" Crown my Saviour King of kings ! "

MAGDALENA.

" Pone luctum, Magdalena ! " — *Latin Easter Hymn.*

MAGDALENA, cease thy grieving,
Cheerful turn thee from thy fears ;
Simon's feast no longer giving
Place for thy repentant tears !
Voices call to gratulation,
Voices call to exultation !
        Hallelujah sound afar !

Magdalena, with new smiling
Let thy lovely forehead glow ;
Where Sin set its hand defiling,
Let the sparkling sunbeams flow.
Has not now the Christ arisen,
Triumphing o'er Death's cold prison ?
        Hallelujah sound afar !

Magdalena, sing thy gladness !
Christ has risen from the tomb,

Finished all the scene of sadness,
Victor He o'er Death and gloom :
Whom in Death thou once wast mourning,
Welcome now in life returning !
      Hallelujah sound afar !

Magdalena, sight amazing !
Lo ! in life thy Lord appears.
Sweet the smile He gives thee, gazing,
View the wounds His body bears, —
Pearls that shine with rays of morning
For the nobler life's adorning !
      Hallelujah sound afar !

Magdalena, droop no longer ;
See thy Sun the darkness part,
Than Death's mightiest power stronger !
Let rejoicing swell thy heart :
Grief and sadness far are driven,
Love and joy forever given !
      Hallelujah sound afar !

AT THE THRONE.

King of glory, crowned for me,
Let me find my strength in Thee ;
Let the sceptre and the throne
Thou dost hold to save Thine own,
Shield me in each trying hour,
Guard me from temptation's power !

Cleansed from guilt, yet sinful, I
Send to Thee my feeble cry !
Strength of earth can never bear
That dear cross I fain would share ;
In Life's dark and dreary way
Thou alone must be my stay.

Naught but need is in my call ;
Simply at Thy feet I fall :
Sick, I seek eternal health ;
Poor, I pray for lasting wealth ;
Blind, I cry to Thee for light, —
Jesus, Master, give me sight !

While around me press my foes,
While no truce the battle knows,
When the valley dark appalls,
Where the King of Terror calls,
King of Glory, crowned for me,
Let me find my strength in Thee !

THE NATION'S JUBILEE.

A. D. 1865.

PEACE, peace ! A grateful nation sings
Her song of songs to-day ;
To Thee, O Lord ! the praise she brings,
To Thee she kneels to pray.
God is our Refuge, still the same !
He maketh wars to cease.
Exalt Jehovah, praise His name
Who grants the people peace !

Peace, peace ! the joyous anthems rise
On peals of music sweet,
Like smoke of ancient sacrifice
Before the mercy-seat.
From bowered hamlets fresh and fair,
From toiling cities grim,
To heaven listening angels bear
A land's thanksgiving hymn.

O God ! we thank Thee that the crown
On Freedom's holy brow
From sea to sea shines radiant down,
Undimmed in lustre now.
Where once the darkness seemed to lie,
We trace Thy wondrous plan,
That taught us never to deny
The brotherhood of man.

We praise Thee from the harvest-field,
Where bent the golden grain,
For every blessing Thou didst yield
To toiling hand and brain.
Each needful store of hard-won gold .
Thy goodness gave, alone ;
Oh, teach us never to withhold
From Thee, our God, Thine own !

We bless Thee for the earthly love
Which cheers our onward way,
As, gathered from the paths they rove,
The dear ones meet to-day.
And mingling round the festal board,
With home-joy in the heart,

To Thine own poor incline us, Lord,
To act the brother's part.

But when, beside the evening hearth,
The saddened memories come
Of hands which never more on earth
Will clasp our hands at home, —
For happier homes beyond the sky,
Beyond these changing years,
As Faith lifts up the raptured eye,
We praise Thee, midst our tears!

O Prince of Peace! whose cross of woe
Our noblest peace has given,
Whose sceptre rules our hearts below,
And guides our steps to heaven,
As Thou didst lead the chosen band
Who sought of old this shore,
So bless with peace this favored land,
One nation evermore.

THANKSGIVING HYMN.

LORD of earth and worlds above,
Thou whose name of names is Love,
Former of this mortal frame,
Guardian of its vital flame,
Bow Thine ear as we would raise
Grateful songs of thankful praise !

For the blood-bought way to heaven,
For Thy grace so freely given,
For the Spirit's life within,
Cleansing from the stain of sin, —
Hear thy ransomed children raise
Grateful songs of thankful praise !

For the months with mercies bound,
For our fields with harvests crowned,
For the glowing flush of health,
For the honest store of wealth, —
Hear Thy toiling children raise
Grateful songs of thankful praise !

For the friends we still retain,
For the homes which yet remain,
For each loved and loving pair,
Centres of the circle there, —
Hear Thy happy children raise
Grateful songs of thankful praise !

For Thy blessings in disguise,
Winning us from earthly ties,
Pointing to Thy home of rest
Where our dear ones still are blest, —
Hear us, Father, softly raise
Grateful songs of thankful praise !

Naught of worth in us we own
As we stand before Thy throne ;
Goodness shines, our needs above,
From the Lord whose name is Love.
May that constant goodness raise
Lives devoted to Thy praise !

VERSIONS OF THREE HEBREW PSALMS.

I. THE HAPPY MAN.

THRICE blest the man whose feet ne'er press
The pathways of ungodliness ;
Who stands not in the way of woe
Where bolder sinners, reckless, go ;
Who sits not where the hardened hear
The mocker's jest, the scorner's sneer !

As blooms the tree within the vale
Whose leaf ne'er fades, whose fruits ne'er fail ;
While constant streams the gifts bestow
Of life and beauty as they flow, —
So prospers he who, day and night,
Finds in Jehovah's law delight.

But like the chaff whose empty form
Is driven by the windy storm
From off the beaten threshing-floor,
To mingle with the wheat no more, —

So flee the wicked from the path
Where sweeps Jehovah's gathered wrath.

They fall before His judgment-seat,
No more with righteous souls they meet ;
For well Jehovah can approve
The narrow way His people love, —
While the broad road the wicked share
He turns to darkness and despair.

II. MESSIAH'S THRONE.

MESSIAH's throne ! Messiah's throne !
A subject-world its sway shall know,
Though kings the sceptre may disown,
And princes plot its overthrow.
Against the Lord they lift their hands,
With hateful rage their strength array :
" Come, let us break Jehovah's bands,
And fling His feeble cords away."

Messiah's throne ! Messiah's throne !
Above the strength against it hurled,
He, whom the calm, broad heavens own,
Laughs all to scorn a rebel world.

His eyes its inmost counsels see,
His voice, deriding, speaks the words :
" My King, on Zion set, shall be
The King of kings and Lord of lords."

Messiah's throne ! Messiah's throne !
Who reigns thereon speaks God's decree :
" From all eternity, My Son,
The earth Thy heritage shall be.
Thy plea shall distant heathen bring
To own Thee as the Lord of all ;
And broken like a worthless thing
Shall every foe before Thee fall ! "

Messiah's throne ! Messiah's throne !
Ye strong and wise, true wisdom learn,
Jehovah-Jesus serve alone ;
With fear and faith to Him return.
Bow, ere His calls of mercy close ;
Bow, ere His anger blasts in flame !
For blest, thrice blest, are only those
Who put their trust in His great name !

II. MESSIAH'S THRONE.

SECOND VERSION.

WHY are the heathen raging
Against Messiah's throne,
Their kings and lords engaging
That sceptre to disown?
On high, Jehovah, scorning,
Derides their hostile will:
"My King, that throne adorning,
Is set on Zion's hill."

To Jesus speaks the Father:
"Thou art th' eternal Son;
Thy royal hands shall gather
The gift Thy prayer hath won.
The heathen's strength before Thee
Shall dashed in pieces be,
And Thou shalt reign in glory
To earth's remotest sea."

Be wise, then, men of power,
To Jesus yield to-day;

Seek peace in mercy's hour,
Ere wrath beset your way.
Bow while His love is pressing ;
Fear, lest His anger flame ;
For blessing, only blessing,
Crowns those who trust His name.

III. ECCLESIA VINCTA, SED INVICTA.

BESIDE thy rivers, Babylon, thy captives sit and weep,
Upon the drooping willows hang the harps that silent
    keep ;
For we remember Zion low, while our enslavers throng
To bid us sing in mirthful joy our once belovèd song.

Sing in the land of strangers far Jehovah's glowing strain !
Forget thee, O Jerusalem, while distant from thy pain ?
May these right hands forget their skill, these tongues
    forget to move,
When we love not Jerusalem beyond our highest love !

Remember, God of Israel, as we can ne'er forget,
The day when in Jerusalem rejoicing foemen met !
How hateful Edom's clamor rose, Destroy, destroy it all ;
Till palace, home, and temple fair to the foundation fall !

O Babylon ! above thee hangs Destruction's cloud of
  gloom.
Happy, as thou hast brought to us, who brings to thee
  thy doom ;
Happy the ruthless hands which slay, as thou didst slay
  our own,
And dash thy children, as our babes, against the savage
  stone !

THE NOBLER HOME.

Not here, 'mid scenes however dear,
 Find I my lasting home ;
The radiant sun holds weariness and death,
The hot plain glows my toiling feet beneath,
The shadows cool stay not upon the path
 Where day by day I roam.

Not here, where falls the frequent tear,
 Find I my lasting home ;
Where trusting hearts are oft asunder rent
As friendships fail, in hopeless striving spent,
Where joys, that flash from far a bright content,
 Vanish like billow foam.

Not here, beset by many a fear,
 Find I my lasting home ;
So often tempted from the narrow way,
So often wandering from that path astray,
So oft despairing, on some gloomy day,
 Lest sunlight never come.

More fair, within a purer air,
    My lasting home I find ;
Promised by Lips which never framed deceit,
Prepared by Power which never knew defeat,
Glowing with Love beyond all love complete,
    Around my Lord combined !

O Night ! pass quickly — for the light
    Of day eternal gleams —
From His dear Face which human pain has known,
But waiting now to welcome to His throne,
From saints who find the rest supreme, alone,
    Surpassing all our dreams.

THE BLESSED DEAD.

THEY have passed beyond our vision, the loved and lost
    of earth,
They have gained the high fruitions of heaven's second
    birth ;
No longing turns their raptured eyes to earth's brief,
    fevered day,
For Life in rarest beauty shines untainted by decay.

They gaze upon their Father 'mid the glories of His
    throne,
They are changed into His image, and know as they
    are known ;
While His wondrous love grows grander within each
    pardoned soul,
As tides of lower oceans fill each inlet as they roll.

They are gazing on their Saviour with ever-new delight, —
That Face desired so often when they walked by faith,
    not sight ;

They see the Brow once crowned with thorns, the
    wounds for sinners made,
They hear the Voice which spake in storms : " 'T is I, be
    not afraid ! "

Around them throng the loved ones who before them
    passed to light,
Whose graves made earth the lonelier, and dimmed its
    glory bright.
Oh, the rapture of the greeting where Death can
    never part !
Oh, the sweetness of reunion of loving heart to heart !

They run to holy ministries as Jesus leads the way,
They feel no toil or weariness, no sun to smite by day ;
From glory unto glory brought, they pass the endless years,
While God's eternal beauty in a constant youth appears.

Blest spirits of the glorified, your happiness supreme
Shines far beyond the measure of our fancy's wildest
    dream.
Though homes of earth are desolate, we cannot crave
    return,
But to share your full redemption our hearts within us
    burn.

DEDICATION HYMN.

LORD of the worlds below, above,
Whose glories shine beyond compare,
To Thee, whose Name of names is Love,
We consecrate this house of prayer.

Saviour, whose human Feet once trod
The pathway of our grief and shame,
Thou dear Redeemer ! Lamb of God !
Write on our work Thy blessed Name.

This make Thy temple, here Thy throne
Establish in the coming days,
As seeking hearts Thy presence own
And kindle as they speak Thy praise.

And as the genial sun and shower
Bring fruitful blessings to the field,
So, Holy Spirit, come with power
To make Thy Word the harvest yield.

Our Fathers' God ! Thy praises still
Shall from these holy courts ascend,
Till we Thy service here fulfil,
And rise where praises never end.

OCCASIONAL VERSES.

OCCASIONAL VERSES.

THE KINGDOM OF HOME.

Dark is the night, and fitful and drearily
Rushes the wind like the waves of the sea ;
Little care I as here I sing cheerily,
Wife at my side and my baby on knee !
 King, King, crown me the King !
Home is the Kingdom, and Love is the King.

Flashes the firelight upon the dear faces,
Dearer and dearer as onward we go,
Forces the shadow behind us, and places
Brightness around us with warmth in the glow.
 King, King, crown me the King !
Home is the Kingdom, and Love is the King.

Flashes the love-light, increasing the glory,
Beaming from bright eyes with warmth of the soul,

Telling of trust and content the sweet story,
Lifting the shadows that over us roll.
 King, King, crown me the King!
Home is the Kingdom, and Love is the King.

Richer than miser with perishing treasure,
Served with a service no conquest could bring,
Happy with fortune that words cannot measure,
Light-hearted I on the hearthstone can sing :
 King, King, crown me the King!
Home is the Kingdom, and Love is the King.

THE WIZARD OF SCOTLAND.

[Read at the Sir Walter Scott Centennial Celebration, Newark, New Jersey.]

FAR from the busy, dusty town
The summer sun shines softly down
Upon a hillside, where the breeze
Frolics amid the sportive trees,
The brook sings merrily along,
While birds send back responsive song.
But mark the stripling in the shade,
Whose length upon the sward is laid, —
With hat thrown back, with jacket torn,
A rustic lad in life's fair morn.
Hard has he fared, I ween, each day
Plodding the dull and rugged way
Which toilers, now beneath the sod,
For generations past have trod.
But now the birds may sing in vain,
The Present holds nor joy nor pain.

A book he reads, and hour by hour
His spirit feels its magic power.
Freed from the bondage of to-day,
Through ages past it wings its way.
He looks on men and cities strange,
On court and camp and moated grange ;
And joys and sorrows, melts and burns,
As page by page absorbing turns.

He lifts his eyes : what shadows pass,
Evoked as from enchanter's glass !
The roads, the hills, the valley seem
Changed as within a wondrous dream.
Lo ! up the mountain path ascends
A Knight, without his squire or friends,
Lost in the wild wood yesterday,
Seeking the stag to bring to bay.
And now, as flashes on the sight
A ruddy watchfire's sudden light,
Rings out the challenge loud and clear
Of an upstarting mountaineer, —
Ah ! soon he knew a foeman near.
What need to tell the boy the names
Of Roderick Dhu and James Fitz-James ?

He turns ; a castle grim and gray,
Like eagle watching for its prey,
Gazes with restless, sleepless eye
Through casement and o'er turret high.
Across its drawbridge like the wind
One rides as Death were close behind.
He wheels, he shakes his gauntlet back
At foe unseen upon his track.
The rider? who but *Marmion bold*
Daring the Douglas in his hold.

The scenes roll on ; and now he sees
An Abbey fair 'mid circling trees.
Without, behold a warrior ride
As in hot haste from Borderside ;
Within, he hears a chanted song
Rolling the pillared aisles along.
The moonlight falls ; its softening beam
Silvers the walls, the trees, the stream,
And through the oriel window glows
Where sleep the great in *fair Melrose.*

Once more is wrought the magic change,
And by its transformation strange

Within a crowded street he stands,
Greeting with silent eyes the bands
Of citizens and ladies gay,
Who sweep, like shadows, on the way.
Past homes so strongly built and high,
The stony form of castle wall,
The city's warder, he can spy,
And faintly hear its bugle call.
But see !   From out the castle-gate
Who fares with retinue of state ?
The *gloomy Morton ;* close to-day
Must faithful friends beside him stay,
For *Mary* rides a Queen again,
And traitors gather in her train.

Another change : the crowds between,
Who clanks along with careless mien ?
'Tis *Claver's !* mark the murmur roll,
" The blood of saints be on his soul ! "
He passes.   Hear the bagpipes fill
The breezes with their whistles shrill.
Hark, hark ! the proud, exultant strain :
" The King shall have his own again ! "
To Holyrood the Prince they bring :
Dun-Edin, out your banners fling.

He comes, he comes with form of grace,
The winsome heir of Stewart's race.
See close attendant at his side
How Bradwardine and Fergus ride.
The watcher starts, — then falls a cloud,
Enfolding as in ghastly shroud ;
The pageants, like the mist, are gone :
The lad lies on the hill alone.

Yet in his life one mighty hand
Has henceforth bid those pageants stand
Linked with reality to bless,
To comfort in all weariness.
No tainted page with devilish art
Corrupts the conscience or the heart ;
The world he treads is nobler grown,
He lives in life beyond his own.
So would he join the praise which tells
Of him who wrought those wondrous spells,
And crown him now with glad delight
   King of the realm of Fancy bright,
   Master amid the men of mind ;
Then turn to thank, with heart aflame,
The God from whom that genius came,
   For sending SCOTT to humankind.

AU REVOIR.

As where the quiet waters sleep
The distant stars draw nigh,
To shine within that mirror deep
As 't were a lower sky, —
So in this quiet, lonely way,
From loving eyes apart,
Thine image glows with fairest ray
Within thy lover's heart.

Yet as those stars beneath the stream
Shine coldly to the view,
And lift us to the warmer beam
That lights the welkin blue, —
So Memory's image mocks desire,
Which soars in fancy free
Past laggard hours to the bliss
When I shall gaze on thee.

Creep on, ye moments ! treasured love
Knows not the word despond ;

O'er time and space, like carrier-dove,
It grasps the rest beyond.
The soul, unwearied in its flight,
While doubt and darkness lower,
Sees from afar the radiant light
Which marks the meeting hour.

BABY SUE.

HAVE you seen our Baby Sue?
With dimpled chin and eye of blue,
Tiny mouth to pout for kisses,
Earnest gaze, which nothing misses
In the narrow world around her,
Where the sights and sounds confound her, —
Cooing, crying, sober, smiling,
All our care and time beguiling?

Nothing of the past she knows,
Strangely every face must greet her,
Not a stream of memory flows
Past the little lotus-eater;
For the present only caring,
In its shade and sunshine sharing,
Clinging to the love that 's dearest,
Grasping at the joy that 's nearest.

What your value, Baby Sue?
Who could guess it if we knew;

Who could give it, would we take it ;
By what calculation make it ?
Diamonds flashing far their brightness,
Ocean pearls of purest whiteness,
Gems and gold from mount and river, —
For them all we would not give her.

But to One whose love bestows
This new life for tender keeping,
From whose Hand each blessing flows
In our joy and in our weeping, —
At His call we hold our treasure,
With her worth past earthly measure,
Praying for His high befriending
Here and in a life unending.

Then we dread not future years
When these dainty feet may weary,
When these eyes may dim with tears
As the world grows dull and dreary.
So we sing as close we hold her,
God still closer doth enfold her ;
Love unfailing hath her keeping, —
Hush ! for Baby Sue is sleeping.

TO MY MOTHER.

[On her entrance upon her seventieth year.]

How bright the days when buds unfold
   Their freshest beauty to the eye,
When groves the mating songsters hold,
   And brooks go babbling by.

Yet into brighter months they pass,
   As summer sheds a warmer glow ;
'Mid flush of song and greener grass
   The streamlets stronger flow.

But fairest of them all the days
   When reapers by the river roam,
And sweet though autumn's golden haze
   Rings out the Harvest Home.

So loveliest shines on us who meet
   A life long past the charm of youth,
Enriched, by toils through summer heat,
   With faith, content, and truth.

It gleams in these fruition years
    Fairer than lives the world has known, —
Through eyes where, often dimmed with tears,
    Love's constant light has shone,

Daughter and wife and mother, wise
    For every service on thee prest,
To-day thy grateful children rise
    And call their mother blest !

University Press: John Wilson & Son, Cambridge.